A QUILT
WITH A
DIFFERENCE

by Trish Puharich
photographs by Adrian Heke

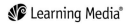
Learning Media®

CONTENTS

1. PLANS FOR THE SCHOOL

We wanted to brighten up our school. We decided that each class would do some artwork. We would work as a team to make our school look awesome.

Our class decided to make a patchwork quilt – with a difference!

A quilt is a cover made from several pieces of cloth that are joined together.

A quilt usually goes on a bed. Some people hang them on the wall or over a couch.

We didn't have any cloth or thread, so we used paper and special printing ink instead. We made a printed quilt! This is how we made it.

WHAT DO WE NEED?

On Monday, Mrs. Mason helped us to make a list of the materials that we would need.

What We Need

- thick cardboard
  thin cardboard
  white and colored
    paper
  printing ink
  rollers and paint trays
- newspaper
  glue
  scissors

Each of us made a piece of the quilt. There are twenty-four children in our class, so we figured that our quilt would have twenty-four pieces.

Mrs. Mason told us about special quilt shapes, like feathers and stars. Then she gave us a design brief. A design brief tells you what something should look like.

Design Brief

Your piece of the quilt must have:
- two different math shapes
- two different quilt shapes.

We carefully read the design brief to make sure that we knew what our quilt piece should look like.

Then we had to decide which shapes we wanted to have on our piece of the quilt.

We made this **checklist**:

Quilt Design Checklist

Name: Michael _ _ _ _ _ _

MATH SHAPES
A four-cornered shape ☑

A closed curve ☑

A three-cornered shape ☐

QUILT SHAPES
A feather ☑

A heart ☐

A star ☑

We checked two math and two quilt shapes on our checklists. Then we put our lists on the wall where we could see them when we were making our printing **blocks**.

What Is a Printing Block?

A printing block is made up of different shapes that are glued onto a base to make a design or picture. The block is covered with paint or ink. Paper is put on top to make a **print** of the design.

3.

STEP BY STEP

On Tuesday, Mrs. Mason showed us how to make a block.

STEP 1

Cut some squares, all the same size, from the paper and from the thick and thin cardboard.

We cut paper and cardboard into squares. (We traced around **templates** to make sure that the squares were the same size.)

STEP 2

Draw some **draft** shapes onto paper.

I looked at my checklist. I drew some four-cornered shapes and closed curves. I also drew some feathers and stars.

I tried drawing the shapes in different ways. Then I had to decide which ones I would use for my block.

STEP 3

Make a good copy of the shapes on the thin cardboard.

On Wednesday, we copied our best shapes onto thin cardboard.

STEP 4

Cut the shapes out and arrange them on the thick cardboard. (Try arranging them in different ways until you like the pattern.)

We carefully cut around the edges of our shapes.

Then we arranged our shapes on our cardboard squares.

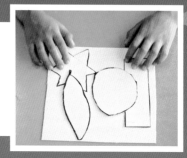

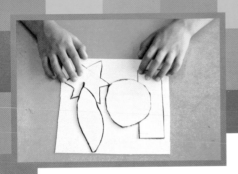

My shapes looked like this when I started ...

and like this when I'd finished!

We glued our shapes onto our thick cardboard squares and left them to dry overnight. Our blocks were ready for printing!

4.

TIME TO PRINT

On Thursday, we got ready to print. We put on our painting shirts and set up four tables with:

- newspaper
- printing ink
- **rollers**
- ink trays
- white and colored paper.

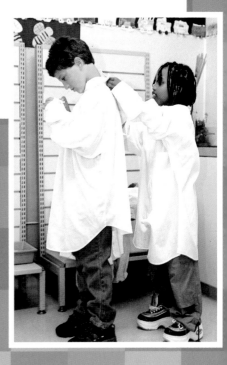

Mrs. Mason showed us how to use our blocks to make a print.

Now we were ready to make our own prints.

My friend Jessie and I chose the green table. Jessie squirted some green ink into the ink tray. I pushed my roller through the ink until it was evenly covered.

Then I pushed the roller backward and forward over my block.

STEP 7

Put the paper on top of the block. Roll over the top and then lift the paper off.

I put a piece of white paper over my block. I made sure that the corners matched up.

I used a clean roller to roll firmly over the top of my paper.

5.
A PRINTING PROBLEM

I peeled my piece of paper away from one corner and looked at my print. Jessie did the same.

Jessie's print had clear edges.

My print didn't!

Mrs. Mason came over to take a look.
"Whoops! You didn't roll right to the
edges," she said. "Come back to the
green table and try again."

So I did. I was careful to roll right to the edges this time.

My second print was perfect! It had two different math shapes and two different quilt shapes. I had followed the design brief.

Excellent!

6.
A Big Success

On Friday, Mrs. Mason brought a huge piece of cardboard into class. We arranged our prints like quilt pieces on the cardboard. We made sure that all the sides and corners joined up.

STEP 8
Glue all of the pieces together to make a quilt.

Then we glued them on.

Our quilt with a difference was finished.

We helped Mrs. Mason to put our quilt on the wall.

Our patchwork quilt sure does brighten up the place! Now the school is looking great because we all worked together as a team.

Glossary

(These words are printed in bold type the first time they appear in the book.)

checklist: a list of items or things to be done

draft: a rough copy

print: a copy of a design made with ink or paint

roller: a round shape used for pressing or smoothing

block: a shape that copies are made from

template: a thin board used as a guide for cutting

INDEX